STUDY GUIDE

I BLEW IT!

Copyright © 2023 by Brian Dollar

Published by Arrows and Stones

Originally published in 2012 by Influence Resources, in association with The Quadrivium Group—Ft. Lauderdale, Florida

All rights reserved. No portion of this book may be reproduced, stored in a retrieval system, or transmitted in any form or by any means—electronic, mechanical, photocopy, recording, scanning, or other—except for brief quotations in critical reviews or articles, without prior written permission of the author.

Unless otherwise specified, Scripture quotations marked NIV are taken from the Holy Bible, New International Version®, NIV®. Copyright © 1973, 1978, 1984, 2011 by Biblica, Inc.™ Used by permission of Zondervan. All rights reserved worldwide. www.zondervan.com. The "NIV" and "New International Version" are trademarks registered in the United States Patent and Trademark Office by Biblica, Inc.™

For foreign and subsidiary rights, contact the author.

Cover design by Anne McLaughlin, Blue Lake Design
Cover photo by Aaron Stone

ISBN: 978-1-960678-34-8   1 2 3 4 5 6 7 8 9 10

Printed in the United States of America

STUDY GUIDE

I BLEW IT!

The biggest mistakes I've made in ministry...
and how you can avoid them

BRIAN DOLLAR

ARROWS & STONES

CONTENTS

Chapter 1. "I KNOW WHERE I'M GOING AND HOW TO GET THERE" 6

Chapter 2. "THIS IS GONNA BE GREAT!" 10

Chapter 3. "THERE'S A KEYSTONE COP AT JESUS' TOMB!" 14

Chapter 4. "HI HO, SILVER!" 18

Chapter 5. "US VERSUS THEM" 22

Chapter 6. "MY LEAD PASTOR JUST DOESN'T GET IT" 26

Chapter 7. "I CAN'T SEE A THING" 30

Chapter 8. "I CAN'T TRY THAT!" 34

Chapter 9. "I'LL TAKE CARE OF THAT TOMORROW" 38

Chapter 10. "I CAN DO THIS ON MY OWN" 42

Chapter 11. "WHERE DO I GO FROM HERE?" 46

Chapter 12. TURN THE PAGE 50

CHAPTER 1

"I KNOW WHERE I'M GOING AND HOW TO GET THERE"

My mistake: Accepting God's destination but forging my own path to get there.

READING TIME

As you read Chapter 1: "'I Know Where I'm Going and How to Get There'" in *I Blew It!*, review, reflect on, and respond to the text by answering the following questions.

REFLECT AND TAKE ACTION:

What are some problems that can happen when we assume we know God's plan without even asking Him to show us?

Why do some of us treat God like a "specially attentive waiter"?

When was a time when you genuinely delighted in God? What was going on? How did it affect your relationship with God, your relationships with others, and your motivation to serve Him?

> *Trust in the LORD with all your heart*
> *and lean not on your own understanding;*
> *in all your ways submit to him,*
> *and he will make your paths straight.*
> *—Proverbs 3:5-6*

Consider the scripture above and answer the following questions:

How often do you lean on your own understanding instead of God's? Why do you think we fall into the habit of doing this?

_____
_____
_____
_____
_____
_____
_____
_____

Have you submitted to the Lord in all your ways? If not, what areas of your life do you still need to submit to Him?

_____
_____
_____
_____
_____
_____
_____

What expectations do you have for God's plan, if any?

___

Take a few minutes now to let God speak to your heart about the importance of delighting in Him. If He shows you that you've been trusting in yourself or gotten too busy, thank Him for His forgiveness, and enjoy His love.

CHAPTER 2

"THIS IS GONNA BE GREAT!"

My mistake: Assuming every good idea is a God idea.

READING TIME

As you read Chapter 2: "'This is Gonna Be Great!'" in *I Blew It!*, review, reflect on, and respond to the text by answering the following questions.

REFLECT AND TAKE ACTION:

What are similarities and differences between a good idea and a "God idea"?

_____
_____
_____
_____
_____
_____
_____

What is the most common reason you settle for good ideas?

_____
_____
_____
_____
_____
_____

Which of the six questions seems most helpful to you at this point? What difference will it make?

_____
_____
_____
_____
_____
_____
_____

> *Pride goes before destruction,*
>
> *a haughty spirit before a fall.*
>
> *—Proverbs 16:18*

Consider the scripture above and answer the following questions:

In your own words, what is the meaning of this verse?

_____
_____
_____
_____
_____
_____

Have you ever let pride take root in your heart? What was the result?

_____
_____
_____
_____
_____
_____

Do God's plans always defy human logic? If not, how can you tell if you're settling for comfortable plans or reaching for faith-stretching ones?

_____
_____
_____

Have you ever mistaken a good idea as a God idea? What was the result?

How do you defend against pride? What is the danger of pride when it comes to God's calling?

In your own words, how can you distinguish between a good idea and a God idea?

CHAPTER 3

"THERE'S A KEYSTONE COP AT JESUS' TOMB!"

My mistake: Allowing my greatest strength to become my biggest liability.

READING TIME

As you read Chapter 3: "'There's a Keystone Cop at Jesus' Tomb!'" in I Blew It!, review, reflect on, and respond to the text by answering the following questions.

REFLECT AND TAKE ACTION:

How have you seen a person's greatest strength become a liability?

_____
_____
_____
_____
_____
_____
_____

What are your God-given strengths? What is the dark side of each one?

_____
_____
_____
_____
_____
_____
_____

How would you define humility?

_____
_____
_____
_____
_____
_____
_____

> *Yet now I am happy, not because you were made sorry, but because your sorrow led you to repentance. For you became sorrowful as God intended and so were not harmed in any way by us. Godly sorrow brings repentance that leads to salvation and leaves no regret, but worldly sorrow brings death.*
>
> *—2 Corinthians 7:9-10*

Consider the scripture above and answer the following questions:

How does sorrow lead to our repentance?

_____
_____
_____
_____
_____
_____
_____
_____
_____

How would you explain the difference between worldly sorrow and godly sorrow?

_____
_____
_____
_____
_____
_____
_____
_____

What are the differences (in focus, feelings, and results) between worldly sorrow and godly sorrow?

_____
_____
_____
_____
_____
_____
_____
_____

What are some lessons you can apply from this chapter?

_____
_____
_____
_____
_____
_____
_____
_____

CHAPTER 4

"HI HO, SILVER!"

*My mistake: Trying to be the Lone Ranger
instead of building a team.*

READING TIME

As you read Chapter 4: "'Hi Ho, Silver!'" in *I Blew It!*, review, reflect on, and respond to the text by answering the following questions.

REFLECT AND TAKE ACTION:

What are some excuses you've heard (or said) for a pastor or leader being a Lone Ranger?

_____
_____
_____
_____
_____
_____
_____

Which of the benefits of a team seem most attractive to you? Explain your answer.

_____
_____
_____
_____
_____
_____

What are your strengths in recruiting a great team? What skills do you need to sharpen? What difference will it make to improve in those areas?

_____
_____
_____
_____
_____
_____

> "His master replied, 'Well done, good and faithful servant! You have been faithful with a few things; I will put you in charge of many things. Come and share your master's happiness!'"
>
> —Matthew 25:21

Consider the scripture above and answer the following questions:

What do you think this verse means? What can you learn from how the master communicated with his servant?

_____

_____

_____

_____

_____

Who on your team is ready to be put "in charge of many things" as a result of their faithfulness?

_____

_____

_____

_____

_____

As you look at your existing team, who are the FAT CATS? Who are the ones who can become FAT CATS with a little time, attention, and training? Is there anyone who just doesn't fit and isn't open to your input?

_____

_____

_____

What's the one thing you need to focus on to build a better team?

What would you rate your current team on a scale of 1-10? How can they better assist you? How can you better equip and empower your team?

1 2 3 4 5 6 7 8 9 10

How do you communicate vision to your team? Why is this important?

CHAPTER 5

"US VERSUS THEM"

*My mistake: Having tunnel vision
and missing the big picture.*

READING TIME

As you read Chapter 5: "'Us Versus Them'" in *I Blew It!*, review, reflect on, and respond to the text by answering the following questions.

REFLECT AND TAKE ACTION:

How have you seen a leader's tunnel vision have negative effects on a team?

_____
_____
_____
_____
_____
_____
_____

Have you ever been a leader or team member in a silo? If so, what happened?

_____
_____
_____
_____
_____
_____
_____

What are some practical steps you can take to avoid tunnel vision?

_____
_____
_____
_____
_____
_____
_____

> *He looked around at them in anger and, deeply distressed at their stubborn hearts, said to the man, "Stretch out your hand." He stretched it out, and his hand was completely restored. Then the Pharisees went out and began to plot with the Herodians how they might kill Jesus.*
>
> —Mark 3:5-6

Consider the scripture above and answer the following questions:

Do you see tunnel vision at work in this passage? On who?

_____
_____
_____
_____
_____
_____
_____

How do you think this situation would have changed if the Pharisees' perspective shifted?

_____
_____
_____
_____
_____
_____
_____
_____

Think about a time you experienced tunnel vision. What were you focused on? What did this prevent you from seeing? How did you fix the problem?

_____
_____
_____
_____
_____
_____

Which of the tunnel-vision-prevention strategies discussed in this chapter are you currently utilizing?

_____
_____
_____
_____
_____
_____

Do you ever feel like you are against other people/groups within your organization? Explain your answer.

_____
_____
_____
_____
_____
_____
_____

CHAPTER 6

"MY LEAD PASTOR JUST DOESN'T GET IT"

My mistake: Ignoring my responsibility to develop a healthy relationship with my lead pastor.

READING TIME

As you read Chapter 6: "'My Lead Pastor Just Doesn't Get It'" in *I Blew It!*, review, reflect on, and respond to the text by answering the following questions.

REFLECT AND TAKE ACTION:

Describe your relationship with your pastor? What are the strengths? What causes frustration (for both of you)?

_____
_____
_____
_____
_____
_____

In your role as a staff member, how do you feel (thrilled, valued, used, neglected, etc.)?

_____
_____
_____
_____
_____
_____

Look at the list of principles in this chapter. Which ones are you doing well? What are the positive results you see?

_____
_____
_____
_____
_____
_____
_____

> *Whatever you do, work at it with all your heart, as working for the Lord, not for human masters, since you know that you will receive an inheritance from the Lord as a reward. It is the Lord Christ you are serving.*
>
> —*Colossians 3:23-24*

Consider the scripture above and answer the following questions:

How can you better embody working with all your heart in your current position?

_____
_____
_____
_____
_____
_____
_____
_____

Do you work for others, or for the Lord? Explain your answer.

_____
_____
_____
_____
_____
_____
_____
_____

Which ones need some work? What specific steps will you take to implement one or two of them? What can you expect to happen? Is it worth the effort?

Do you need to have an honest conversation with your pastor about your role? How will you prepare for it? When will you have it?

How do you support your pastor? Which of the methods mentioned in this chapter do you employ?

CHAPTER 7

"I CAN'T SEE A THING"

My mistake: Being blind to my weaknesses and flaws.

READING TIME

As you read Chapter 7: "'I Can't See a Thing'" in *I Blew It!*, review, reflect on, and respond to the text by answering the following questions.

REFLECT AND TAKE ACTION:

What are some blind spots you've noticed in people's lives? Why haven't they been honest and courageous in dealing with them?

_____
_____
_____
_____
_____
_____

Has God shown you a blind spot in your life in the past few years? What did you do when you saw it?

_____
_____
_____
_____
_____
_____

What has the Spirit whispered to you as you read this chapter? Are you eager or afraid to hear Him?

_____
_____
_____
_____
_____
_____

> *For we live by faith, not by sight.*
> —*2 Corinthians 5:7*

Consider the scripture above and answer the following questions:

In your own words, what is the meaning of this verse?

_____
_____
_____
_____
_____
_____
_____

What will your life look like and how will it change when you start living entirely by faith?

_____
_____
_____
_____
_____
_____
_____

What is your next step (or first step) in dealing with the blind spot in your life? Who can help you?

_____
_____
_____

Do you think remedying your weaknesses is a process or a one-time event? Explain your answer.

When was the last time you went to God in humility and asked Him to show you your weaknesses? What was the result?

Why is honesty the first step to overcoming weaknesses and flaws?

CHAPTER 8

"I CAN'T TRY THAT!"

My mistake: Allowing fear to keep me from taking risks.

READING TIME

As you read Chapter 8: "'I Can't Try That!'" in *I Blew It!*, review, reflect on, and respond to the text by answering the following questions.

REFLECT AND TAKE ACTION:

What are some ways fear cripples people, ruins relationships, and keeps us from doing what God has called us to do?

_____
_____
_____
_____
_____
_____

What fears are problems for you? How do they affect you?

_____
_____
_____
_____
_____
_____

Which of the principles in this chapter encourages you most? Which one terrifies you?

_____
_____
_____
_____
_____
_____

> *For the Spirit God gave us does not make us timid,*
> *but gives us power, love and self-discipline.*
>
> *—2 Timothy 1:7*

Consider the scripture above and answer the following questions:

When have you demonstrated a spirit of timidity in the face of uncertainty or fear?

_____
_____
_____
_____
_____
_____
_____
_____
_____

When have you demonstrated power, love, and self-discipline in a difficult situation? How can you respond like this every time?

_____
_____
_____
_____
_____
_____
_____
_____
_____

What are some steps you can take to downsize and crowd out your fears?

_____

_____

_____

_____

_____

_____

_____

_____

_____

CHAPTER 9

"I'LL TAKE CARE OF THAT TOMORROW"

My mistake: Falling into the procrastination trap.

READING TIME

As you read Chapter 9: "'I'll Take Care of That Tomorrow'" in I Blew It!, review, reflect on, and respond to the text by answering the following questions.

REFLECT AND TAKE ACTION:

What are some reasons a lot of ministry leaders don't prepare well? Which are good reasons, and which are excuses? How can you tell?

_____
_____
_____
_____
_____
_____
_____
_____
_____

What are some benefits of good preparation and communication with a team? Are these benefits worth the effort? Why or why not?

_____
_____
_____
_____
_____
_____
_____
_____
_____

What changes do you need to make in your planning, preparation, and communication with your team? When will you make this happen?

When was the last time you let procrastination get the better of you? What was the result?

How do you and your team defend against procrastination?

What is your team's current system of preparation? How could this system be improved upon?

CHAPTER 10

"I CAN DO THIS ON MY OWN"

My mistake: Becoming self-reliant instead of trusting God to use me.

READING TIME

As you read Chapter 10: "'I Can Do This on My Own'" in *I Blew It!*, review, reflect on, and respond to the text by answering the following questions.

REFLECT AND TAKE ACTION:

What does it mean to be "broken and contrite"? Why does it take the work of God's Spirit for this to happen in our lives?

_____
_____
_____
_____
_____
_____
_____
_____
_____

Have you experienced genuine brokenness? As you read this chapter, did you sense God was pointing out some area of your life that isn't fully surrendered to Him? If so, how would you describe the problem?

_____
_____
_____
_____
_____
_____
_____
_____
_____

How would you answer these questions: Am I pursuing God more passionately than I'm pursuing anything else, including God's work? Have I empowered people to speak into my life?

_____
_____
_____
_____
_____
_____
_____

> *To this end I strenuously contend with all the energy Christ so powerfully works in me.*
>
> *—Colossians 1:29*

Consider the scripture above and answer the following questions:

What do you think Paul meant when he wrote this verse?

_____
_____
_____
_____
_____
_____
_____
_____
_____

Do you work with or against God and His guidance? Is this always the case? Explain your answer.

_____
_____
_____
_____
_____
_____
_____
_____
_____
_____

Do you want a broken and contrite heart? Be honest.

_____
_____
_____
_____
_____
_____
_____
_____
_____
_____

Talk to God about your answer.

CHAPTER 11

"WHERE DO I GO FROM HERE?"

My process: Learning to confess, repent, and reconcile.

READING TIME

As you read Chapter 11: "'Where Do I Go From Here?'" in *I Blew It!*, review, reflect on, and respond to the text by answering the following questions.

REFLECT AND TAKE ACTION:

Author Phillip Yancey calls forgiveness "the unnatural act" because everything in us cries out to get even. Do you agree or disagree with his assessment? Explain your answer.

_____
_____
_____
_____
_____

Look at Colossians 3:12-15. What happens when we try to follow those directives without experiencing Christ's love, patience, kindness, and forgiveness at a very deep level?

_____
_____
_____
_____
_____

What are some reasons excusing, minimizing, and denying often seem so much more attractive than forgiveness? When we lean in one or more of these ways, what happens to the guilt (if we're the offender) or the resentment (if we're the victim)?

_____
_____
_____
_____
_____

> *Therefore, as God's chosen people, holy and dearly loved, clothe yourselves with compassion, kindness, humility, gentleness and patience. Bear with each other and forgive one another if any of you has a grievance against someone. Forgive as the Lord forgave you. And over all these virtues put on love, which binds them all together in perfect unity.*
>
> *—Colossians 3:12-14*

Consider the scripture above and answer the following questions:

How can someone clothe themselves with all the traits that Paul mentions in this passage?

_____
_____
_____
_____
_____
_____
_____

Why does Paul say to put love above all else? Are you doing this in your life?

_____
_____
_____
_____
_____
_____
_____

Which of the three components of an apology seems hardest to you? Explain your answer.

Why is it important to realize that forgiveness is both an event and a process—both for the offended and the offender?

Has the Holy Spirit prompted you in any way as you read this chapter? If He has, what's your next step?

CHAPTER 12

TURN THE PAGE

My commitment: Moving past the past.

READING TIME

As you read Chapter 12: "Turn the Page" in I Blew It!, review, reflect on, and respond to the text by answering the following questions.

REFLECT AND TAKE ACTION:

Do you and your family observe any New Year's traditions? If you do, how effective are they? If you don't, how might it help to begin them?

_____
_____
_____
_____
_____
_____
_____
_____
_____

When was a time you had the courage to turn the page in your life, leaving the past behind and reaching forward to something better? What were the circumstances? How did it work out?

_____
_____
_____
_____
_____
_____
_____
_____
_____

What are some ways a significant failure or being deeply wounded can make us prisoners of the past? What are some reasons we stay there?

_____
_____
_____
_____
_____
_____

> *"Can a mother forget the baby at her breast and have no compassion on the child she has borne? Though she may forget, I will not forget you! See, I have engraved you on the palms of my hands; Your walls are ever before me."*
>
> *—Isaiah 49:15-16*

Consider the scripture above and answer the following questions:

How do these verses make you feel? How do you think you'll act differently if you dwell on what God says in these verses?

_____
_____
_____
_____
_____
_____
_____
_____

What do you think "walls" means and represents in this passage?

_____
_____
_____
_____
_____
_____
_____
_____

All of us have heard cutting words that sandpaper our confidence. What are some messages you've heard? How have they affected you?

_____
_____
_____
_____
_____
_____
_____
_____

Which of Moses' doubts and excuses sound like something you might say to God if you were in his position? How did God respond to each one?

_____
_____
_____
_____
_____
_____
_____

What would it mean for you to turn the page—today—toward a better future?

_____
_____
_____
_____
_____
_____
_____

www.ingramcontent.com/pod-product-compliance
Lightning Source LLC
Chambersburg PA
CBHW070050100426
42734CB00040B/2973